[1001 photographs]

Dogs

[1001]
[photos]

[1OO1] photos

Dogs

©2006 Copyright SA, France
©2007 Rebo International b.v., Lisse, Netherlands

This 2nd edition reprinted in 2008.

Concept and realization: Éditions Solar
Editors: Françoise Huart and Ségolène Roy
Editorial coordination: Isabelle Raimond with Lise Chantelauze and Léa Chantereau
Graphic design: Gwénaël Le Cossec
Photography: Frédéric Bar
Typesetting: A.R.Garamond, Prague, Czech Republic
Translation: First Edition Translations Ltd, Cambridge, UK
Proofreading: Erin Ferretti Slattery

ISBN 978 90 366 2249 3

Dogs
[**1001**]
[photos]

REBO
PUBLISHERS

Contents

Companion Breeds

Sheepdogs

Sight-hounds

Terriers

Sled Dogs

Hunting Dogs

Water Dogs

Watchdogs

Companion Breeds

The Yorkshire Terrier came to be thanks to the endeavors of miners who were trying to develop a dog for rat hunting so tiny that it could fit into a pocket.

The Chihuahua has the immense privilege or handicap, depending on one's viewpoint, in being the tiniest dog in the world. Its name is derived from the name of the Mexican province from where it originated. Aztecs adored the Chihuahua but at the same time they prepared from it one of their popular meals ... the Chihuahua has sparkly eyes and thanks to its big ears it looks as if it is constantly alert.

It is always on the move and compensates for its small body with a sharp voice. Admittedly it cannot face large enemies or dangers, but can draw attention to the tiniest risk and that is why it is also called the "dog-hooter." The Chihuahua is a resilient dog, which can adapt to all climates. This "pocket-sized" pet is devoted, loyal, and even possessive. It is intelligent and hates being alone.

The Basenji is of South African descent and its origin undoubtedly dates back deep into the ancient era. It is also called the Congo Terrier. In Africa it was used to track prey in the bush and as a hunting dog. Its sense of sight and smell are exceptional. It displays a calm and devoted character.

The Yorkshire Terrier is a relatively new breed, which was developed in the Yorkshire County of England. It is a well-known dog with a pony-tail in its hair. Owners often treat it like a doll. In English "high society" this dog was promoted among aristocrats, whereas before it was an ordinary rat hunter in mining regions. Today it is a palace dog

Chihuahua, Basenji, Yorkshire Terrier and King Charles

par excellence. The Yorkshire Terrier is stubborn and when attacked will respond to the challenge. This playful and cuddly terrier loves the company of children and just like children the Yorkshire Terrier can also be unpredictable and capricious.

Despite its small size, the Chihuahua is a strong and sturdy dog. Thanks to the increasing popularity of this dog, its breeding intensified, which however resulted in a certain deterioration of the skull structure that has become fragile. The fontanel of Chihuahuas never closes.

The Basenji hardly ever barks, with the exception of one type of sound, which resembles laughter. On the other hand, this dog communicates very expressively with facial gestures and body movement.

In the 19th century, Scottish miners, for whom poaching was often vitally important, used Yorkshire Terriers to flush rabbits out of their burrows century. They tried to give it longer hair by crossing it with the Bichon Maltese to make it easier to pick the dog up quickly if they were caught red handed.

The coat of the Yorkshire Terrier is long, straight, shiny and of a soft and silky texture requiring everyday grooming.

The Cavalier King Charles Spaniel owes its origin to breeders who wished to revive and reintroduce an old type of Toy Spaniel which was popular with English Kings in the 17th century.

This little companion, which is very popular in Great Britain, is very lively and has qualities suitable for short hunts in flat terrain. Nevertheless it also shows a liking for comfortable living.

The Cavalier King Charles
Spaniel is admittedly of
a robust constitution, but
it dislikes cold and damp.

The King Charles Spaniel of Spanish origin lived in England as early as 1870. This dog was named after Charles II (1630-1685), who would never part from it. At that time this breed had a longer nose and was larger than today.

The Standard and Miniature Poodles are admittedly of a controversial origin (France, Denmark, Germany or Italy), however they bear a French hallmark. Their name in French, *caniche*, is derived from the word *canichon*, which referred to a duckling as well as the dog that hunted it. The poodle directly represents the canine race: a loyal companion, groomed with a foppish hairdo, spoiled by its masters, acting in a merry, obedient and playful way.

The Dalmatian did not originate in Dalmatia and despite its name it definitely is not a Yugoslav. This dog and its numerous offspring became very popular thanks to the Walt Disney film – *101 Dalmatians*. There are a lot of hypotheses as to its origin. This breed probably came from Asia, by way of Egypt and Greece and in the 18th century it arrived in England. It has many abilities: it proved its worth as a messenger in Dalmatia during the Balkan War, moreover as a guard dog, sheepdog, guide dog and even a sled dog. This extremely popular dog has quite the image of an upmarket

Poodle, Dalmatian and Bulldog

The poodle has many talents: from a circus dog to a game hunter, and in between a model for great artists of the Renaissance period. Painters of the 18th century used to paint them in at the edge of the canvas. The poodle is known as one of the most intelligent of dogs, teasing, vivacious, with an excellently developed sense of smell–simply ideal as man's best friend.

dog, connected with aristocracy and old mansions. It is an animal without great initiative, calm, playful with children, melancholic, and has a great need for human company. Its coat is internationally recognizable. Dalmatian puppies are born with pure white coats.

The French Bulldog is, as its name suggests, of French origin. Several stages of cross breeding resulted in a dog with a considerably small body, but with the qualities of a Molosser: a large head and sullen look. However it does not have anything in common with the aggressive Bulldog showing red lips and bared teeth. Its ancestors were brave dogs trained for hunting wild animals and cruel and aggressive fighting dogs. Today, the French Bulldog is a companion dog, likeable, pleasant, exemplarily loyal, loving children, disciplined and calm. Its body is massive with short legs and tensed muscles; it looks as if it is constantly in a defensive position, yet it deeply abides to a family atmosphere and without any doubt its best friend is man.

The Bulldog is of English nationality, but definitely of Asian origin. It is massive, stocky, with a docked tail; rather sinister-looking... this perhaps is due to its past role as a fighting dog combating bulls in an arena. Luckily this unrewarding task has not been expected of it since the 18th century. Nevertheless the Bulldog has remained a police dog, a guard dog and also an excellent companion dog, which regardless of its looks is very placid.

The French Bulldog was used as a rat hunter by shop owners, wine merchants and butchers in slaughterhouses. It was idealized by High Society and as such its popularity quickly spread.

The Bulldog survived the ban on bull baiting in 1835, thanks to selective breeding. This resulted in the development of a more placid dog. However, it unfortunately had to pay for it with frequent health problems.

The ears of puppies of this breed will prick up after a few weeks.

The Poodle's coat changes its color as it grows and it takes about two years before it gets its final shade.

The Poodle shows a great capability to learn; it often performs in circuses, but it can also be used as a guide dog or truffle hound.

In the Poodle there are two coat varieties: curly and twisted, though the latter is rare. Twirls start to form after 9 – 18 months.

At the beginning the "lion haircut" was aimed at making swimming easier for the Poodle and at the same time protecting the heart. Gradually in the 18th century, the once hunting dog from the swamps changed into a "court pet."

The difference between individual Poodle varieties lies in their size. The largest one is the Standard Poodle reaching the height of 16–24 inches.

When born, Dalmatians are as white as snow. The black spots, something of a trademark, appear gradually between the 10th and 14th day.

The Dalmatian, which has boundless energy, was used as a guard dog, sled dog as well as circus dog. In the 19th century it was helping American firemen by guiding the horses, which were pulling the fire engines.

The Chow Chow is a member of the Spitz group of dogs as is, for example, the sled dog the Alaskan Malamute. The slanting eyes, a face hidden in a mass of hair from where only pointed ears and a "squashed like" end of the snout jut out, mostly display a sullen look.

Lacking much exuberance, it obeys the commands only of its master and may act aggressively towards unknown people. It is a dog which owes its introversion probably to the history of its ancestors: in the 18th century the Chow Chow used to pull carts in China and its meat was a delicacy sought-after by emperors as well as simple coolies. ... It loves rice.

dogs! It is an excellent sociable dog, taciturn enough and mistrusting of strangers.

The Pug resembles a miniature Mastiff. It used to live in China and from there it was brought to Europe. Thanks to its square snout and round head with wrinkled forehead it looks both a little terrifying and yet sweet at the same time. Its very black and flat nose is the reason for its deceptive appearance, because the Pug is gentle, devoted, even though a bit distrustful and sometimes aggressive towards strangers. It was a cherished dog of the Marquise de Pompadour, Queen Marie Antoinette and other crowned heads.

Chow Chow, Tibetan Spaniel and Terrier, Pug, Shar Pei

The Tibetan Spaniel is probably more or less related to the Pekinese or the Pug. It has a plumed tail and its ears hang down. Do not mistake this dog for the Brittany or Picard Spaniel, because it has absolutely nothing in common with hunting

The Shar Pei was once a fighting dog in China. Its sad and tired eyes and skin with heavy folds impart it with charm and originality. Everybody agrees that this dog is most unusual.

As the Chow Chow grows it tends to put on weight. A mane appears round the neck.

Chow Chow puppies, real soft teddy bears, can almost be seen to grow day by day. They, similarly as adult dogs, are also considerably indifferent and a little aggressive.

In China the Pug was known under the name *ba guo* ("snorer dog"). Thanks to its flattened face it was nicknamed a pug (from the expression – a pug nose). Its extremely thin nostrils are not very effective in thermal regulation and that is why Pugs are extremely sensitive to heat.

The Tibetan Spaniel
[2, 5] is a breed of a
very old origin, which
was used by Tibetan
monks for turning
the prayer wheel,
but served also
as a guard dog.

This shepherd, which the English mistakenly named the "Tibetan Terrier" [1, 3, 4, 6, 7], guarded horses, sheep and yaks. It can pride itself on being a companion of Tibetan monks, because according to tradition, people instead of killing the weakest of the litter, were supposed to give it to monks.

The Shar Pei is a level-headed, calm dog, greatly devoted to family members. It loves children and shows amazing adaptability. This dog is obedient, disciplined and an excellent guard worth the everyday training required.

The Shar Pei became world renowned after making it into the *Guinness* Book of *Records* in 1978 as the rarest dog in the world. Its wrinkly skin, sunken eyes, miniature ears and head resembling a hippo justify the attention they receive from lovers of oddities.

The Shar Pei was originally used as a hunting and guard dog and later also for fighting purposes. It would have died out during the era of the revolutionary Peking regime that had banned the ownership of dogs if it had not been for the moving of the last remaining animals, which lived in Hong-Kong, to the United States.

The name Shih Tzu comes from the Chinese, where it means "lion." The Chinese used to respect this dog even more because they worshiped the lion as the king of beasts. This dog appeared in Europe in the 1930s and its popularity peaked in the 1950s.

With its body this breed resembles the Lhasa Apso and with its snout the Pekinese. It is a stay-at-home dog that loves a luxurious and sterile environment. Yet it is vivacious and playful.

The Petit Brabançon is a strange mixture. It has something from the Schnauzer, something from the Pug, as well as the Affenpinscher, and a tiny beware: it does not enjoy the company of small children!

The Pomeranian is a miniature descendant of the Giant Spitz originating from Germany. The breed was developed by the English: it used to be four times bigger than it is today. It is an excellent guard, as well as a loving and loyal pet.

The Mexican Hairless Dog is one of the oldest known breeds because its origin dates back to 1500 BC. According to Aztec mythology it was named "Xoloitzcuintle," the earthly representative of the god "Xolotl," which accompanied the dead to the underworld. In the past it was also used as a hot-water bottle, and was a great help

Shih Tzu, Petit Brabançon, Mexican Hairless Dog, Pomeranian

bit from the Yorkshire Terrier... It is a little, outgoing dog, which often looks as if it is in a bad mood, but more times than not it behaves as a pleasant, obedient and devoted pet. Thanks to its rather gremlin-like appearance the Petit Brabançon looks interesting and friendly. But

for problems of rheumatism and pain because its body temperature is 40 °C, two degrees higher than in most other dogs. The Mexican Hairless Dog is always on the lookout and is mistrustful of strangers, which makes it a good guard dog and an excellent companion.

The sacred task of the Mexican Hairless Dog (Xoloitzcuintle), did not save it from being consumed by Indians because in their opinion it was very delicious meat.

Bald smooth skin is the main genetic feature of the Xoloitzcuintle. However, this "Toy" breed can also have some hair.

Contrary to the Belgian and Brussels Griffons, which have quite a stiff coat, the Petit Brabançon has short fawn or red hair, often with a black mask, or a black coat with reddish highlights.

Queen Victoria, enchanted by this intelligent and lively little dog, started the craze for Pomeranians in the 19th century.

The Shih Tzu admittedly shows a certain independent character, but at the same time it is affectionate and grateful when being looked after.

As a puppy, owing to its fluffy fur, the Shih Tzu looks like a soft toy. When it rests, it makes a characteristic purring.

The Coton de Tuléar originates
from a town of the same
name on the south coast
of Madagascar.

The Bichon Maltese, despite its name, did not come from this island in the Eastern Mediterranean but places far more distant, as believed by some experts, from the Asian continent. However, the breed was developed in Italy and was named "Melita" after an island in the Adriatic Sea.

Nevertheless, everybody agrees that it is one of the oldest breeds, known before Christ: a guard dog in Egypt, a popular lap dog for ladies of Athenian nobility during the era of Ancient Greece and one of the favorite companions of Francois I and a member of the court of Louis XV. The silky appearance and pure white color of its coat impart this breed with its characteristic image: a luxury dog reserved more for women clientele. Incidentally, ladies love it when they can pamper this dog, doll it up, or comb and decorate it with tiny pink bowknots. The Bichon Maltese is a placid and obedient, loyal and non-aggressive dog, which has excellent hearing that makes it alert to the slightest noise.

The Bichon Havanese is of a more unclear origin. Italian-Maltese? Argentinean- Caribbean? Or a bit of everything? No matter how it came to be, one thing is certain, it is a rare and totally companionable breed of dog.

The Coton de Tuléar is of Madagascan origin. It is related to the Bichon Maltese, and excels as a great companion dog, a good swimmer and walker.

The Little Lion Dog is a result of crossing the Bichon Maltese with the Water Spaniel and perhaps the Spaniel. Its known roots date back to the 15th century. This breed owes its name to

Bichons, Coton de Tuléar and Little Lion Dog

its mane, which resembles the type that adorns a lion. The Little Lion Dog is robust, full of energy, cheerful and intelligent. This breed hardly exists outside of France, Belgium and Great Britain and has been become rarer and rarer of late.

The Coton de Tuléar has a cotton-ball-like coat with long, soft and slightly frizzy hair. The fur is white and sometimes, contrary to the European Bichon, has yellowish markings, mainly on the ears.

Even though the Coton de Tuléar looks fragile, it is a sporty dog that loves training and walks. This dog needs everyday combing, otherwise its coat gets matted.

Thanks to the traditional "lion style" haircut, this Little Lion Dog can look fragile, though in fact it is sturdy and a bigger dog will not make a great impression on it.

The Bichon Maltese, depicted on the famous tapestry "Lady and the Unicorn," has always been admired by prominent people of this world. It is not advisable to judge it solely on its noble appearance, because it is an untiring and tough dog.

The Bichon Havanese possesses all the qualities of a companion dog: it is likeable, sensitive and much attached to its master. It can give the impression of being timid.

The Bichon Havanese is no longer in favor in Cuba and is gaining newfound popularity in the United States.

White fur is quite rare in the Bichon Havanese. This dog is usually more or less fawn, grey or its color is a mixture of these shades. Its long and wavy hair tends to form locks.

As its name suggests, the Bichon Bolognese comes from Bologna, northern Italy. This dog has a great resistance to heat.

The Bichon Frise, which was a popular
pet of Francois I, gave new meaning to
the French word "bichonner" that originally
meant "to curl the hair"; it is now used
in the sense of "to preen oneself."

The Dachshund shows
affection as much
as obstinacy and courage.

D achshunds originate no doubt from the Basset. Even though the Dachshund is of German nationality, it is a very old breed, whose traces can be found on Egyptian sculptures. There are three varieties of Dachshunds of various sizes and type of hair: long-haired, smooth-haired and wire-haired.

Looking at their bodies, one could easily say it is a "toy" dog. In fact it is an excellent dog for flushing prey out of a burrow, specialized in badger hunting! However, people know and see it as a companion dog, which is "energetic," obstinate, slightly full of itself, a little capricious and jealous. Despite the bad points, their masters spoil them and let Dachshunds dominate them – this mischievous companion can use its charms with no shame whatsoever. In the way in which its theatrics and mood swings are excused, the Dachshund is unrivalled.

The Welsh Corgi is of Welsh nationality. Usually it is classified among herding dogs; it has been used for this purpose since the end of the Middle Ages. Even before that it was employed as a hunting dog. Due to its short and stocky build, people associate it with the Bassets. However, this smallish dog combines in itself the qualities of a shepherd, guard and companion dog. Corgis are also a part of the English royal court, because the Queen chose them as her "favourite" dogs and never leaves her Pembroke Corgis behind. Apart from the Pembroke Corgi,

Dachshund and Pembroke Welsh Corgi

there is another Corgi breed, called Cardigan, with a long tail and short hard coat: greatly resembling a fox. On the other hand the Pembroke hardly has a tail at all. Both these breeds of the Welsh Corgi are calm, affectionate, dynamic and intelligent.

The coat of a Dachshund (here the smooth-haired variety) changes at the age of 2 months. Dogs with black or light brown coats will keep their colors, whilst a red coat will become brighter and creamy shades will turn into golden or reddish hues.

Thanks to its well developed sense of smell the Dachshund was used for badger hunting. Its name in German, *Dachshund* means "badger dog." The so-called "Kaninchen" type, which is a German word for rabbit, was used for flushing rabbits out of their burrows.

The wire-haired variety of the Dachshund was developed by crossing Terriers and Schnauzers.

The Dachshund's bark is surprisingly low, but powerful: that is why it is necessary to teach it self-control right from the very beginning.

The long-haired Dachshunds resulted from crossing with Spaniels.

81

A typical feature of the Welsh Corgi-Pembroke which is a cousin of the Cardigan, is the absence of a tail, which explains its rather waddling way of walking.

The Lhassa Apso,
originating from Tibet,
appeared in France
as late as 1949.

T he Lhassa Apso of Tibetan nationality is an odd mixture of the Terrier and Tibetan Spaniel. Its name is derived from the town of Lhassa, where this dog lived in Tibetan monasteries performing its role as a guard dog. In the past it was sacred but today its role has been reduced to a more mundane one: that of a lap dog.

Thanks to its well developed sense of hearing it can warn against imminent threats. The Lhassa Apso is a cheerful, lively and self-confident dog.

The Miniature Pinscher is a variety of the Pinscher, which is a blend of the Schnauzer, Doberman and obedient and not very bulky, so it has all the qualities of a companion dog.

The German Pinscher as the name suggests is of German nationality and undoubtedly of a very old origin. In the presence of strangers it barks aggressively though it is not nasty. However its voice is very dissuasive. This dog combines the qualities of a watchdog and a companion dog.

Lhassa Apso, Miniature and German Pinscher, Miniature Schnauzer

Manchester Terrier. It is not much bigger than the Chihuahua, has a pointed muzzle, a very black nose and pointed ears. It is also called a "roebuck" or "dwarf." This breed is not very popular in France, but sought after in Germany and Switzerland. Thanks to its relationship with Terriers it is an excellent rat hunter. The Miniature Pinscher is robust,

The Miniature Schnauzer comes from Bavaria, Germany. It acquired its name thanks to its characteristic nose (Schnauze means "snout" in German). In the past these dogs lived in stables with horses fulfilling the role of a hunter of rats, field mice and other rodents. It has remained a very good guard dog, which at the same time is devoted and intelligent.

The name of this dog probably comes from the Tibetan expression *lhasa apso seng kye*, which means "a lion dog of Lhassa that barks well." According to a different etymological explanation its name refers to the golden colored fur, resembling the hair of a Tibetan goat, which in Tibetan is *apso*.

The Lhassa Apso, which was kept in lamasseries and considered to be a sacred animal, appeared in Europe late because it was prohibited to sell these animals.

This long hair
needs grooming
everyday and
bathing once
or twice a week.

The Miniature Pinscher [1, 2, 3, 4] is often mistaken for the Miniature Doberman or the Chihuahua. The German Pinscher [5, 6, 7] requires a lot of exercise and has a tendency towards fighting.

The Miniature Schnauzer is a vigorous dog, easy to train and occupying minimum space.

The Papillon is a variety
of the Continental
Toy Spaniel.

The Pekinese is probably the ancient Chinese "Pa," which according to legend was born out of the love of a lion and a monkey. From the lion, it inherited nobility, and from the monkey its appearance. This dog was the sole property of Chinese Emperors and for 15 centuries it was kept in the Forbidden City! After the death of its master, it was sacrificed.

And maybe it is just this ancient status of a mythical animal and sacred dog which today gives it its slightly condescending appearance, its noble and light gait. It is a luxury dog that loves comfortable interiors, silky cushions and the pompom slippers of its mistress, because the Pekinese is very appreciated by ladies. This is one of the oldest dogs in the world (undoubtedly more than 4, 000 years old). It displays no aptitude at all for sports and shows itself as a dog attached to the house and its master.

The American Cocker Spaniel was developed from the English Cocker Spaniel. Originally, it was a hunting breed, but today it is a companion dog, capable of chasing game, and which has maintained its enjoyment of running. It is cheerful, obedient and intelligent. This breed became famous thanks to the Walt Disney animated film *Lady and the Tramp*.

The Continental Toy Spaniel has been known since the Middle Ages. In the 16th and 17th century it was a frequent guest at royal and aristocratic courts, appearing in paintings by Rembrandt, Rubens and Vélasquez. The "Phalene" version with dropped ears is older than the "Papillon" type with erect ears that appeared in the 19th century. This dog loves an audience and has a theatrical talent. It can often be seen in circuses.

Pekinese, American Cocker Spaniel, Continental Toy Spaniel and Eurasier

As said by some of the owners, Pekinese puppies behave very strangely: "At the age of one or two months they will let you do what you want. You can turn them onto their backs and they will not try to roll back – they will stay as they are, sprawled on their backs looking at you with complete trust."

The ears of this miniature Spaniel, which tremble like butterfly wings, will prick up when the puppy is aged between the 3rd and 4th month. When born, the coat is predominantly black and brown, but gradually these colors fade away giving way to white.

The Papillon was developed in the 19th century by crossing with the Small Spitz.

The Eurasier was developed in Germany in the 1950s by crossing the Wolf Chow and Samoyed. It is cheerful, even-tempered, loyal and simply perfect in its role of a companion dog.

[1, 2 and 3] The American Cocker Spaniel is smaller than the English Cocker Spaniel, from which it descended, but its coat is more sumptuous and varied.

102

[4 and 5] The Phalene has dropped ears. Similarly as with the Papillon, its rich, long and wavy coat does not need any special care.

Sheepdogs

The Collie has a great sense
of the family, it is happy only
in the shadow of its master.

The Briard, also known as Berger de Brie, is currently very popular in France and also outside its borders. Its origin is undoubtedly very ancient. Traces of its existence can be found as early as the 14th century in *The Hunting Book of Gaston Phebus* and some paintings of the Italian Primitives dating back to the 15th century.

It is a dog of rural appearance, surprisingly agile and lively, with a contrasting personality: a remarkable guard of herds and an amiable companion. This "James Bond" of the dog world was used as a dispatch bearer during World War I. It can be used as a guide dog as well as for rescue work in mountains. The Briard is intelligent, gentle and greatly dotes on its master.

The Collie is sometimes also called the Scottish Long-haired Shepherd. It is undoubtedly a product of odd crossings between Scottish dogs, sheepdogs and greyhounds. This beautiful dog was made immortal thanks to the role of Lassie, the most typical example of a Collie of fawn color, with the typical mane and frills. It is gentle and sensitive, but can also be nonchalant and sometimes sad. Admittedly it copes well with cold and rain, but on the other hand it cannot stand heat very well. The Collie becomes enthusiastic in open spaces.

The Bearded Collie was originally an excellent herding dog, like its close and distant relatives, such as other types of Collies, the Bobtail or Briard, with which it shares a number of physical similarities. Thanks to its unique sense of smell, initiative and intelligence it is a particularly talented sheep

Briard, Collie and Bearded Collie

herder. It also obtains excellent results at the "Dog Agility" contest. The Bearded Collie has become a British dog par excellence. Its existence in the British Isles including Scotland is substantiated from the 16th century. It is assumed that it was brought to Great Britain probably at the time of the Roman conquest.

The Collie is very easy to train, which is why it is well suited for obedience and "agility" trials. It needs vast open spaces and adapts poorly to living in an apartment.

As Collie puppies grow, their snouts stretch out and the color of their mane intensifies.

111

Berger de Brie is an efficient and independent dog capable of guarding a herd of 200 – 300 animals entirely on its own. Today with the number of animals in herds on the decline the Briard is less in demand.

The Briard was developed by crossing the Beauceron and the Water Spaniel. It has small, high positioned eyes covered with long hair. Its coat is long, dry and supple.

The coat of Bearded Collie puppies brightens up after 6 months and one year later it gets its definitive color, with the exception of the black coat. In the end the big eyes are fully covered by hair.

The Bearded Collie has a thick coat that protects it from the damp chill of the Scottish Highlands, where it often used to stay on its own with a huge flock of sheep.

T

he Pyrenean Shepherd, or Labrit, is considered a veteran among French sheepdogs. It has three varieties – the Rough-faced type, which is the most widely known and is undoubtedly an offspring of the Great Pyrenees, the semi-rough and the Smooth-faced Pyrenean Shepherd with a long snout.

This is a dog perfectly adapted to a mountainous region. The Pyrenean Shepherd is intelligent, authoritarian and sometimes distrustful, and can win respect from animals, mainly horses. Thanks to its exceptionally developed sense of hearing, it is an excellent guard dog. During World War I, owing to its shrewdness and sense of smell, it was used as

The Maremma and Abruzzes Sheepdog is undoubtedly one of the oldest breeds of herding dogs. Its origin dates back hundreds of years. Today, the Maremma and the Abruzzes Sheepdogs are considered to be the same breed and therefore referred to with a united name. This dog with a pure white coat has a lively and intelligent look. While working with herds it is a perfectionist, nothing goes unnoticed and it can even behave aggressively against herd enemies, both people and animals. It is used to large areas and dislikes being shut indoors, but

Pyrenean Shepherd, Maremma and Abruzzes
Sheepdog, Polish Lowland Sheepdog, Polish Tatra Sheepdog

a dispatch bearer, similarly as the Briard. This breed will easily become attached to its masters and children, so it is a very reliable companion dog, from which however it might be necessary to "erase" the characteristics of a dog used to large areas.

its kind and adaptable nature make it a good companion, if it has the chance of a good run around. It is a robust dog, with good immunity against diseases. It will adapt to all types of food, but will not turn down a meat dish!

The Pyrenean Shepherd is very efficient and is used for herding cattle, but mainly sheep. Its task is to gather the animals, lead and separate them as well as to find strays.

The Pyrenean Shepherd has distinctive, black-circled dark brown eyes. It has long hair on the head and face.

The Polish Lowland Sheepdog, or as referred to in Poland "Nizinny," has an excellent memory, which makes training simple. This breed also displays an excellent sense of observation.

The Maremma and Abruzzes Sheepdog is a part of the group of large herding dogs originating from the East, similarly as for example the Hungarian Kuvasz or Komondor.

The Polish Tatra Sheepdog, a relative of the Hungarian Kuvasz, is not afraid of wolves or bears. It is exceedingly sure footed thanks to which it can accompany animals in an undulating terrain.

The Groenendael Belgian Shepherd is a relative of the German Shepherd. Its distinguishing feature is its black shiny coat. The name of this breed comes from a chateau of the identical name located not far from Brussels. This dog has an elegant gait; from the 15th century it was accustomed to living at royal courts.

It is a multifaceted dog and one needs to know what this breed is suitable for – it is a sheepdog, guard dog, search-and-rescue dog in avalanches and a tracker. It clings a lot to its master, adores children and has problems if its family surroundings are changed. This dog is as unpredictable and choleric as it is gentle and affectionate. In view

The Tervueren Belgian Shepherd was developed in the Brussels quarter of the same name. It resembles the long-haired German Shepherd. It is more robust than the Groenendael and similarly as other Belgian Shepherds it has an excellent sense of smell. Thanks to this quality and its great ability to learn it is a renowned working dog, used for searching in avalanches, as a messenger and rescue dog. The Tervueren also helps blind and handicapped people.

The Lapinkoira, or Finnish Lapphund, is one of the oldest known breeds. Laplanders used it for guarding half-tamed foxes. Outside Finland it is valued as a companion dog

The Vastgotaspets or Swedish Vallhund is popular in Sweden. It is brave, independent and extremely

Belgian Shepherds - Groenendael and Tervueren, Lapinkoira, Vastgotaspets

of the fact that this breed is quick-tempered, if you do not know the particular dog well it is better to approach it carefully.

talented in sports and therefore it needs space and cannot adapt to living in an apartment, although it is valued as a companion dog.

Several years are necessary for the creation of the beautiful coat of the Tervueren with long thick hair of the desired length.

The Lapinkoira coat covers various shades of grey-black and fawn color with markings.

The Groenendael is one of the varieties of the Belgian Shepherd, the others include Laekenois, Malinois and Tervueren.

Similar to the Tervueren, the Groenendael is sensitive and suited to an extreme environment.

The corded coat
of the Komondor has
always protected it
against adverse weather
conditions and wolf bites.

T hanks to its thick and corded fleece, which looks as if it was made from raw wool, the Komondor does not resemble any other dog. Its muzzle cannot be seen at all, which brought it the nickname "dark and handsome stranger." This dog is rustic, faithful and brave; it does not fear the job of guarding the herd and moreover it is also an exceptional security dog. It is not afraid to test its strength against wolves, the animals it knows only too well.

this type of dog is touchy and sulky, hidden behind a wall of hair, which reaches into its eyes. Despite being an excellent companion dog it needs training and fresh air.

The Bobtail or also the Old English Sheepdog or even the English Dog with a short tail is, as to its origin, probably a distant relative of shepherds which were probably brought to England from Italy during the Roman conquests. However this has never been proven. Today this breed is considered

During the Asian migrations its ancestors faced large predators. Despite its hulking appearance the Komodor's gait is light with a prolonged step. In daytime hours it rests and at night it becomes active. Its look and

Komondor, Hungarian Sheepdog, Bobtail

defensive posture evoke respect and fear. The Komodor's conspicuous teeth appear terrifying. Moreover, it attacks in a silent fashion. It can behave very gently towards children, and police use it as a tracking dog in snowy areas. However,

to be the most English of the British sheepdogs. Its qualities as a shepherd were valued mainly at times when guarding herds and stables was its main task. Nowadays, it is a very sought after companion dog.

It is an exuberant and affectionate dog. Its appearance is admittedly a bit odd, but resembles the Briard, Bergamask, Puli and Komondor. It looks a bit like each of these, with its long hair, thick coat and graceful gait. It is valued as a competition dog and has been many times depicted in paintings by English artists. The Bobtail is a playful dog, which one has to say can behave well, needs a good run-about and also due to its size and temperament is not destined to be a mere "couch dog."

The Hungarian Sheepdog or Puli is very popular in Hungary. For a long time it guarded enormous flocks of sheep in Puszta, large wild plains, which since then have been brought under cultivation. During World War II it almost died out, but luckily survived abroad where some owners moved it, particularly the United States. Today, it is used less as a herding dog as it has adapted well to living in towns.

A Komondor puppy is traditionally brought up among sheep and sheered together with them. In North America it protects young dogs from coyote attacks.

While the puppy's coat is not corded, some ropes of the Hungarian Sheepdog can reach as far as the ground.

The Bobtail has become a greatly valued companion dog, loved mostly by children. It probably transferred its instinct of guarding a herd to watching over kids. With its very peculiar cracked voice it barks only when necessary.

In the past, working dogs differed from luxury breeds in having their tails cut off to avoid the obligation to pay special taxes on them. If the Bobtail is born with a tail, it will be docked in the first days of its life.

When born, Bobtail puppies weigh around 370 – 400 grams (nearly a pound). In the course of one year they will increase their weight a hundred fold. At the age of 6 months their hair is so long that it starts covering their round eyes and one-year old youngsters will acquire thick double hair, leaving behind the shaggy coat of a puppy.

149

The Australian Shepherd,
an excellent companion,
is still very rare in European
countries.

The Border Collie is one of the most formidable sheepdogs. It has been gifted with a delicate sense of smell, an impressive gaze, which can even mesmerise cattle. Its deep rooted disposition is towards caring for herds. That is why it is very unhappy indoors and cannot bear inactivity.

This dog of Scottish origin is tireless and relentless. It is also very sensitive and attached to its master, whose tasks it fulfils to the letter.

The Catalan Sheepdog or Gos d'Atura is closely related to the Pyrenean Shepherd. It has the same pointed ears, the same thick coat and the identical towards its master in an obedient and amiable fashion, which is the quality that makes it a valued companion dog.

The Australian Shepherd really comes from Australia, but it has become a full fledged American breed. Since World War II its popularity has kept on growing thanks to its participation in rodeo, horse races, films and television programs. This dog shows great devotion to a family and is valued on American farms and ranches.

Border Collie, Catalan Sheepdog, Australian Shepherd and Shetland Sheepdog

laughing and expressive eyes. This unkempt dog with a bohemian look is a tireless herd guard as well as a versatile dog, which can be used as a watchdog, police dog or a dispatch bearer. Towards other animals it acts in an energetic manner and

The Shetland Sheepdog originates from islands of the same name to the north of Scotland. It is a small dog, very well adapted to a rough climate. It acts protectively towards children, hates brutality and needs training.

The Australian Shepherd has changed its role from watching over sheep to a search-and-rescue dog.

153

The kind and playful nature of the Australian Shepherd resembles that of the Golden Retriever and Labrador.

The Australian Shepherd guards sheep as efficiently as cattle, which this dog drives with a special cry, something between hooting and barking.

The Shetland Sheepdog is a very intelligent dog, easy to train and at the same time playful and jolly.

The excellent sense of smell of the Border Collie enables it to find the trail of a lost animal, even in the thickest fog.

A Border Collie puppy has the typical coat and nature of its breed from the age of 1 – 2 months.

The obedient Catalan Sheepdog will adapt to all tasks, which it will perform with courage.

The coat of the Catalan Sheepdog is long and rough, straight or slightly wavy. It forms a beard, moustache, forelock and distinctive eyebrows. It has a long tail, which sometimes is docked because of work, but some animals can even be born without one.

The Appenzeller
Sennenhund can be an
excellent sheepdog as well
as a proficient watchdog.

The Bouvier des Flandres, whose appearance is rather forbidding, is an efficient dog par excellence. It was used as a guard and search dog by the police and army, mainly during World War I, due to which it almost disappeared. It is also a cattle guarding dog and a sled dog.

Its sense of smell, intelligence and power are admirable. Despite the thick eyebrows and tangled hair it is an amiable, calm and loyal dog. Even though it is nicknamed "scruffy" due to its unkempt appearance it is one of the best companions for a family environment. Nevertheless you dare not touch anything that is dear to it, because then the

originates from Asian Molossers, which Roman legions used as fighting animals. This dog, distrustful of strangers, but very attached to its master, is beautiful, energetic and intelligent and ranks as one of the best sheepdogs. Thanks to its brilliant memory it is also an excellent rescue dog.

The Appenzeller Sennenhund, or Appenzeller Mountain-Dog, is of Swiss nationality. For a long time it accompanied Swiss peasants pulling carts loaded with goods to markets. It is an excellent

Bouvier des Flandres, Bernese Mountain Dog, Appenzeller Sennenhund

Bouvier des Flandres would show itself as a terrifyingly protective dog.

The Bernese Mountain Dog of Swiss nationality was given the nickname "bear cub." This breed

sheepdog, but also an unrivalled multi-functional dog: a tracker, watchdog and a rescue dog. Compared with other Swiss shepherds its body is relatively small, but it is energetic and tireless, and adapts very badly to an inactive life style.

The tail of the Appenzeller Sennenhund is curled on the side into a spiral, unlike other Swiss sheepdogs.

The Bernese Mountain Dog has a tri-colored coat with black the base color together with rust and white markings. It is made up of long fine hair, which is thick and soft, slightly wavy, but not curly.

The coat of the Bernese Mountain Dog is white on the chest, nose, legs and the tip of the tail.

The coat of the Bouvier des Flandres is wiry and looks a little tousled. It has a soft and thick undercoat, which protects it well against cold and inclement weather

Sight-hounds

The Saluki was probably
a favorite dog
of Tutankhamen.

The Saluki or Persian Greyhound is of Iranian nationality and Asian origin. Without doubt it was imported from Asia by the Greeks and travelled from Italy with the Romans during military campaigns. The Saluki, casually lying on Oriental rugs, is the dog from the fairy tale, A Thousand and One Nights. This dog, a privileged companion of sheiks of the Arabic world, is treated with great respect.

This breed, which Muslims consider sacred, was exempt from Islamic law that regards dogs as dirty animals. In Arabic countries, it is not sold, but given as a token of friendship and respect. It is a good hunter of gazelles as well as being a handsome dog. It needs running exercise every day and almost immediately it can reach its maximum speed, but when hunting it hardly every responds to being called back. It is one of the most beautiful gems among the sight-hounds. This dog is very sensitive, so its upbringing requires a great deal of ingenuity.

The Whippet together with the little Italian Greyhound is the smallest member of this group, something of a miniature greyhound. It is of English nationality. It shares its good points with the sight-hounds: nobility, elegance, gentleness and speed, while it lacks the drawbacks: frailty and size. It is an excellent runner: it can reach a speed of 30 miles/hour. As with all the Greyhounds, the Whippets are used at race tracks. The name of this small racing dog was probably based on the deformed English expression "whip it," used by their masters when encouraging the dogs during

Saluki and Whippet

races which they took part in. Anyway, whippet races are very impressive. Despite its slim appearance, it is a robust, easy-going dog, jolly, sensitive and playful. An ideal companion breed, if you respect its need to have a proper run in the fresh air.

The Saluki puppy moves as if in slow motion, with a graceful gait.

The Saluki, a fast sight-hound, with extraordinary sense of smell and sight was used for hunting gazelles and jackals. Its light movement evokes the impression that it floats.

The Saluki is a great friend of other dog breeds, but towards strange animals they are usually distrustful. Similarly, their exclusive attachment to their master results in them being restrained or even shy in the presence of strangers.

Though born for running
and hunting, with the need
for plentiful exercise,
Whippets are also reserved
and very affectionate dogs.

185

The Sloughi or, the Arabian Greyhound comes from North Africa. It is popular mainly in France, although it is of Moroccan nationality. It is a well muscled, gentle and elegant dog. It is slim, bony and light-colored, thus making it easy to blend in with a sandy environment.

At one time chiefs of Berber tribes used it for hunting gazelles in the desert. Even today Nomads employ this dog for hunting and guarding. It is an intelligent, proud and independent sight-hound.

The Afghan Hound is a very old breed originating from the Middle East which came to England as late as the 19th century. From a wolf and jackal hunter it has become one of the most sought-after and expensive companion dogs. The "Hound in Pyjamas" as it is nicknamed is not necessarily a stay-at-home type! It loves running and movement. One must not forget that this breed comes under the category of hunting dogs.

The Azawakh is of French nationality. It is a variety of the Sloughi, which is more common with Nomad tribes, particularly Tuaregs. In Europe it has been known only since the 1970s. It is slim, large and hyper-muscled.

The English Greyhound is a synonym of elegance and nobility. It is an "Englishman," settled in Great Britain for many years, even though its origin lies undoubtedly in the East, maybe in Greece, because its name was probably the Greek Hound. It is a dog of the English royal court and also a hotshot at races. England, where greyhound races have been run for ages, uses this dog at race tracks for hunting decoys. Nevertheless, it is also a pleasant companion dog.

Sloughi, Afghan Hound, Azawakh, English Greyhound

Afghan Hound puppies reach maturity a little late, after 3 – 4 years, when they acquire a regal appearance, which is the source of their great charm.

Afghan Hounds are intuitive
hunters that have kept their liking
for racing and chases. Therefore,
they do not respond to being called
back very readily and must be
brought up very strictly.

The Sloughi [1-2], which was in its time a favorite with the Berber "aristocracy" is pleasing to the eye with its slim musculature, noble behavior and the nostalgia of its gaze. Its extremely soft skin is covered with a short sandy coat, with or without a black mask, which can have traces of red or brindle.

The English greyhound [3] is an excellent athlete with an aerodynamic silhouette and short, soft, closely fitting hair.

The Azawakh, which is very rare in France, excels with a slender silhouette and the gaze of a gazelle. It is a brilliant hunter, bouncily galloping along.

The Irish Wolfhound is the national dog of Ireland and together with the Great Dane they are the largest dogs in the world.

T he Borzoi or Russian Wolfhound is the largest and the most majestic of all the sight-hounds. Distinguished and slender, it is a noble dog par excellence. This aristocrat of the canine race was, particularly in the 19 century, a favorite companion of Russian Tsars, but also other crowned heads of Europe. It was a companion dog of large imperial families and moreover it was used for hunting bears.

The Borzoi's origin dates very far back; in France it appeared in the Middle Ages. Its majestic gait, and composure give it almost a contemptuous expression. At present, it is mainly a companion dog, so it needs to be taken out for walks and allowed to run about, because it requires a lot of movement. However, the Borzoi is entirely happy during soirees. Its obedient and restrained nature, its beauty and intelligence make it an unrivalled companion.

The Irish Wolfhound or Irish Greyhound can outgrow all the sight-hounds and reach up to three feet in height at the shoulder, which is a result of extraordinary growth. The breeders restored this type of dog by crossing the last remaining animals with Deerhounds and maybe Great Danes, and even today it keeps growing. It has less aristocratic behavior than its relatives. It looks more rustic and immediately reveals its origin as a hunter of wolves, deer and large predators in some countries such as the United States. Nevertheless, in the 18th century, together with the wolf it almost disappeared. It is a peaceful, quiet and loyal dog, and does not have the character of a guard dog

Borzoi and Irish Wolfhound

despite looking like a "tough guy" and regardless of its feared strength. It is neither phlegmatic nor depressive and has a great need for a proper run outside.

With its arched back, deep chest and long, straight muscular limbs, the Borzoi is well balanced and extremely elegant. Its slender silhouette is not affected by wind, and that is why its gait is extremely light.

197

The Irish Wolfhound is strong, well developed, but at the same time supple and agile. Its rough and shaggy coat is grey, black, light to ginger fawn, or light brindle.

Terriers

T he Soft-Coated Wheaten Terrier is of Irish nationality. Its exact origin is not known. However it is regarded as one of the oldest terriers. It is a hunter and therefore it is an ideal dog for the countryside: it likes hunting small animals and guarding property or herds.

It is not the most famous English terrier, but it is an active, courageous and obedient dog, well adapted to living in the countryside. It is called a "Wheaten" because its coat is often the color of ripened wheat. This dog does not often appear at international competitions, but it is a faithful companion to its master.

contented as a companion dog, or thanks to its resonant barking and always-on-guard behavior, as a miniature watchdog.

The Welsh Terrier is a close relative of the Fox Terrier. It is obviously of British nationality, but it has American roots. It is a cross of small terriers

Welsh Terrier, Tibetan Terrier, Black Russian Terrier,
Glen of Imaal Terrier and Soft-Coated Wheaten Terrier

The Tibetan Terrier or the "Chrysanthemum Dog" is probably the ancestor of the Tibetan Spaniel, Lhassa Apso or Shi Tzu. However, it also resembles the Bobtail in a scaled-down version. It is a lively, gentle and amiable dog, which shares with the terrier only its name, because it has never hunted. With its size and abilities this dog is much more

with the Airedale, of which it is an exact scaled-down copy. It has been transformed from a rural dog bred for otter hunting to a companion dog, developed for competitions.

The Welsh Terrier has more than one string to its bow. Its qualities are the qualities of a terrier, but it can adapt itself to a water environment too. It has the aptitudes of an urban dog used to living indoors, children and a quiet life.

The Tibetan Terrier has a thick fine coat, neither silky nor woolly,
which is straight or wavy, covering the soft undercoat.
All hair colors are acceptable, apart from the chestnut shade.

The coat of the Soft-Coated Wheaten Terrier, of light to dark fawn color, consists of rich, soft, wavy or curly hair, where the front locks are large and loose.

The very old breed of the Glen of Imaal Terrier [1 and 3] can hunt rodents. Sometimes it is used for badger and fox hunting. The Black Russian Terrier [2], the largest of the terriers, is a tenacious hunter, resilient to the climate of the country of its origin.

The Cairn Terrier
is the oldest breed
of the Terrier group.

S imilar to the Skye Terrier, the West Highland White Terrier is a Terrier Basset. This dog is also called a "Westie" and it is a white variety of the Cairn Terrier, which in the 19th century appeared in some of its litters. It was bred on farms where it was used for hunting vermin.

This Terrier has a mischievous look, loves the company of people, particularly children, and has an excessive liking for vast spaces and countryside after its ancestors. Quite simply it is an excellent rural dog, valued for its small size and charming nature.

The Skye Terrier is one of the oldest Terrier Bassets. It probably comes from the Isle of Skye, northwest of Scotland. There are several legends told about its history, for example that its origin can be found in the territory of Barbarians or that it is a descendant of the Bichon Maltese which escaped from a shipwrecked Spanish vessel. It is a hunter, watchdog and shepherd, now used by Brits for badger hunting. The Skye Terrier is a courageous dog, whether used as a hunter or guard dog, as well as being a loyal companion that shows a very privileged attachment. Be careful, it is touchy and dislikes being shut in anywhere for a long time. Regardless of its small body and appearance of a "couch dog," do not confine it to an apartment.

The Cairn Terrier is of English nationality and is one of the really small Terriers. It is a rural dog, a good

Westie, Skye Terrier and Cairn Terrier

hunter with a happy, lively and kind nature. Contrary to other Terriers it is not aggressive and does not have a special need to run and hunt. It is a good companion dog, although very obstinate.

The coat of the
Cairn Terrier puppy
is less thick and
more fluffy than
that of an adult
dog. It slowly
thickens, hardens
and changes color.

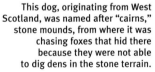

This dog, originating from West Scotland, was named after "cairns," stone mounds, from where it was chasing foxes that hid there because they were not able to dig dens in the stone terrain.

This lively and intelligent dog, the canine star of the *Wizard of Oz*, is an excellent companion for children. The Cairn Terriers are courageous and gifted with a strong character.

216

When born, the puppies of the West Highland White Terrier are totally white, with the exception of the snout and pink paw pads that after 3 – 4 days get covered with black patches and then spread gradually over the entire paws.

The Skye Terrier is a long bodied dog
with short legs and stiff coat, curly
and plaited, of black, blue, grey
and fawn color.

The American Staffordshire
is exceptionally strong
for a dog of its size.

The Boston Terrier is of American nationality. It is a dog of surprising appearance. It is classified in the Terrier group, but it resembles more a small Mollosser, with its wide and flattened face, pointed ears and smooth short coat. Its veins carry the blood of various origins (English Bulldog, Bull Terrier, Boxer and Old English White Terrier), which provides it with a unique character.

At the beginning it was bred for dog fights, which were popular in some American towns. It does not have any of the hunting qualities of Terriers. On the other hand this dog is very courageous, agile and boisterous, and likes playing with adults and children. The Boston Terrier is generous and none too aggressive. In New England, in the United States, it has created for itself the reputation of a real gentleman. It will adapt to small spaces, in the town and country. In brief, it is the "must-have" of the companion breeds, more a toy than a terrier.

The American Staffordshire was developed in the United States in the 19th century from the English Staffordshire Bull Terrier, which was used to fight dogs and bulls. It kept from the English dog its aggressiveness towards other dogs, which can lead to killings due to its very sharp teeth, capable of causing serious injuries. In order to cope with this tendency toward aggression it is necessary to provide the American Staffordshire with the opportunity to stay in the company of other dogs from puppyhood onwards. Despite this characteristic

Boston Terrier, American Staffordshire Terrier

feature, this breed can behave very attentively towards children and adults and show loyalty, intelligence and obedience. Thanks to its good temperament, it is a greatly valued companion dog, which can be also entrusted with a guarding task, because it is courageous, strong and agile.

The American Staffordshire is a dog with a respectable body that demonstrates great suppleness.

The American Staffordshire has a short, thick and shiny coat, rigid to the touch.

223

Due to their flattened muzzle the Boston Terrier puppies have difficulties in sucking their mother's milk and later also eating solids. Until a certain age they also tend to snore.

The Boston Terrier's coat is short, smooth and shiny. The color can be brindle, seal (black with a red sheen) or black with white markings.

The Airedale Terrier is of British nationality as are most of the Terriers. It was named after a river in Yorkshire. Tall, well-built and brawny, the Airedale is fast and always ready for action. It is tireless and impulsive; capable of standing up to much stronger opponents – its close ancestors used to hunt bears and wolves.

Today it will make do with deer, wild boars and badgers. Being gifted, it has been used for many varied tasks: in war as a dispatch bearer, a police dog, guide dog, watch dog, as well as a fighting and hunting dog specializing in otters in marshlands. Today, its breeding focuses mainly on being an excellent companion dog, which plays at tracker in the apartment halls ...

combat-loving and cunning dog, which will not be led by its nose. The Smooth Fox Terrier is a good-natured dog, with a good body constitution. It probably kept the temperament and qualities of the now extinct breed – the Agassin Terrier.

Its relative, the **Wire Fox Terrier,** has the same fighting and hunting nature. It is elegant, brawny and thanks to its beard, a bit of a "dandy." One can see in this dog a slight tendency towards theatrics. Surely for this reason Hergé modelled the Milou Dog, a loyal and cunning companion of Tintin, on

Airedale Terrier, Smooth and Wire Fox Terrier

The British **Smooth Fox Terrier** is a real hunting Terrier, courageous and more of a fighter, fully in line with its distant ancestors. The existence of this dog was recorded as early as Roman times and then in the Middle Ages. It is an independent,

this breed. The Wire Fox Terriers could give a hard time to anyone that would try to stand against them. Their ancient skills and legendary vehemence makes them excellent guard dogs with a hostile bark towards strangers.

The Airedale Terrier is curious, emotional and noisy. It loves chewing things and chases anything that moves. This dog stays playful and mischievous for all of its life.

The Airedale Terrier puppy is black with fawn markings at the end of its paws and eyebrows. As it keeps growing, the coat stiffens and darkens. At the age of 6 months, it already has the coat of an adult.

The Smooth Fox Terrier is the oldest and least common variety. Its coat has to be flat, hard, smooth and dense. The colors match those of the Wire Fox Terrier.

233

Black markings on the face of the Fox Terrier puppy gradually turn lighter resulting in a nice wheat shade at about two months of age.

This courageous and impulsive dog is an instinctive hunter. It can win respect from strangers, but has the unpleasant characteristic of attacking other dogs.

The individual temperament of the Bull Terrier requires strict training right from the very beginning.

The Bull Terrier was developed in 1830 by breeders longing for a dog with the same aggressiveness but better agility than the Bulldog, bred for bull baiting, which then was very popular across the English Channel. At that time the Bull Terrier was a product of crossing the Bulldog with Terriers. As a fighting dog, the Bull Terrier could behave cruelly and in a blood-thirsty fashion. Since then it has become "urbanized."

It has maintained some of the qualities of a quard dog and simultaneously, thanks to the effective selective crossing, it also has gained a more civilized side. However, for the master to be able to make use of it, he must show his physical strengths and apply tried and trusted techniques. The Bull Terrier will submit to discipline, while holding on to its rather stubborn character, displaying an even-tempered nature and behaving towards people in a kind fashion. It is a loyal and unassuming companion dog.

In the past, **the Border Terrier** was used for hunting foxes, which attack lambs, as well as performing the task of guard dog at the Scottish and English border, hence its name. Its ancestors probably include the now extinct English dog - the Dandie Dinmont Terrier and Bedlington Terrier. The adult Border Terrier has a wide skull, large eyes and strong jaws and due to this it resembles an otter. The hindquarters are powerful, as well as the

Bull Terrier, Border Terrier

rear paws, designed for running behind hunters on horse-back. The Border Terrier has a long, but stocky body suited to racing, and needs intensive exercising. It is sociable and easy to train. Thanks to its kind nature, happy temperament and loyalty to its master, it is a companion dog loved by children.

Thanks to its balanced character the Bull Terrier is an excellent companion dog.

The short, smooth, shiny and hard coat is either of pure white, or white with colorful markings on the head, or its coat is multi-colored with white prevailing.

239

Originally fierce, or even scowling, the Bull Terrier is in a way a "gladiator of the dog world," full of fervor and courage.

When born, the Bull Terrier is quite long, but in time its strong constitution takes over.

When the Bull Terrier is instilled
with the necessary discipline,
it becomes an affectionate,
well balanced, stable
and faithful companion.

243

The coat of the Border Terrier consists of a rough thick cover, protecting this dog when hunting in bushes, and a dense water-proof undercoat.

The Jack Russell Terrier has a small body and therefore it is effective at flushing prey out of burrows.

The Jack Russell Terrier is of English nationality. It was named after Reverend Jack Russell, the "creator" of the Fox Terrier, who developed this breed for hunting, mainly as a suitable dog for flushing foxes and other animals from their dens. One has to say that the Jack Russell Terrier is of the ideal size for this job. Flexible joints, dropped ears and white coat stand out distinctively, preventing hunters mistaking this dog for game.

In the Terrier family it is quite an unusual breed. The upbringing of the Jack Russell Terrier must be strict varieties: the larger and stockier Parson Russell Terrier and the longer, shorter-legged Jack Russell Terrier.

The Scottish Terrier is of British nationality, while being a typical Scot. Some hundred years ago it lived in the Western Highlands and the Hebrides. It is of dark color, has a square-head, pointed ears and a beard under its muzzle, its appearance resembling old English colonels. This excellent short-legged hunter is robust, copes well with bad weather conditions and shows signs of stubbornness. However, it tires quickly, and therefore it is important not to set out for long walks with it and watch it very carefully when it plays in water, an activity particularly loved by this dog. The Scottish

Jack Russell Terrier, Scottish Terrier

and start early. It is a courageous dog with no fear, showing enough friendlessness, too. It is necessary to point out that this dog is a born hunter and tends to run after anything that moves. That is why one must make sure that it does not set out chasing cars! The former breed developed into two Terrier is bold, fears nothing, displays the aptitude of a good guard, which surprisingly barks only a little. When brought up properly it is also an excellent companion dog, loved by children. The snobbish expression disguises a joyful and roguish temperament and strong individuality.

Jack Russell puppies are very much alike, but as they grow, they start differing in their height and length as well as their coat quality; their silhouettes can vary quite markedly, too.

The coat can be smooth, hard or even wiry. It is well resistant to foul weather.

The coat of the Jack Russell Terrier is rough, dense and thick, smooth or stiff. It is either of pure white or white with colored markings. In France it is quite rare at present.

Rather long than tall,
the Jack Russell Terrier is born
for speed and endurance.

The Scottish Terrier has a likeable appearance. Its dense, hard, sometimes even rough coat is black, wheaten or light brindle. Its originality is highlighted by its moustache and long eyebrows.

Sled Dogs

The Alaskan Malamute is the best known of the sled dogs. Owing to its half-shut eyes and wide head, children see it as a charming wolf. It is a very strong and resilient animal in perfect harmony with its natural environment: snow, open spaces and extreme cold. It is not as fast as a Husky, but more tenacious, and as such it was selected for dog sled races over short distances.

Moreover, it is a reindeer, seal and bear hunter. It was named after the Eskimo tribe of Mahlemuts. With its way of life and the constant presence of humans, the Alaskan Malamute became attached to the human race, making it an excellent companion dog. It is a strong and courageous animal with a well developed sense of orientation and very acute sense of smell. Apart from the heroes of Jack London's stories it has become a symbol of the adventures of the Far North.

The Siberian Husky is a member of the group of four polar dogs together with the Samoyed, Alaskan Malamute and Groenendael. It was most valued by far for its azure eyes, its energy and exceptional stride when it pulls a sled. For a long time it outshone its close relative the Alaskan Malamute. Originating in Siberia, it appeared in Alaska at the beginning of the 20th century. It is mainly a messenger dog. Affectionate and gentle, it becomes exaggeratedly attached to its master. It can also display some stubbornness. One must respect its need to have a run in open spaces and let off steam. There is a definite no to shutting it indoors. Despite its beauty it is not an ornament. Nevertheless, it is extremely sought after for competitions, for its black – circled blue eyes ...

Alaskan Malamute, Siberian Husky

The Malamute, which has been trained for working in a team, is an affectionate and friendly dog. It excels as a loyal and devoted companion that loves playing immensely.

The thick fur efficiently protects the Malamute against severe cold, it can sleep in snow and ice even in below zero temperatures. In order to protect itself against a snow storm this dog will curl its tail around its muzzle.

The Malamute has "snowshoe-like" paws, because its pads are strong, well padded and separated from toes with a thick line of hair.

The Siberian Husky can adapt to a moderate climate very well. It needs a lot of exercise and that is why it is not a dog suited to an urban environment.

The "mask" on the Husky's face –
especially around the eyes – is highly
distinctive in puppies. Around the age
of 4 to 5 months it begins to diminish
and entirely disappears at the age
of one year.

In English the word "husky" refers to the throaty characteristic sound which this sled dog makes.

The Siberian Husky has a thick double coat. The undercoat is dense and soft in texture. All shades are acceptable, ranging from black to snow white. Markings on the head are of a characteristic shape.

Huskies were developed by Chukchis, a nomadic tribe similar to Eskimos who lived in North Siberia. From there the dogs were brought to Canada by a fur merchant in 1900 to take part in a dog sled race, where they proved their speed and endurance.

The Samoyed, originating from Siberia, was named after Samoyed tribes that used this dog for pulling a sledge and watching over reindeer in the tundra, where it was considered to be a gift from angels. Around 1890 it was discovered by British explorers, who undertook large polar expeditions in the Arctic, and was brought to Great Britain.

This dog with immaculate white fur is used to the barren areas in the north and to demanding tasks. It is of a firm body, and despite its relatively hard and wild life, it is not nasty or aggressive. Thanks to its moderate, warm and obedient temperament it is a wonderful companion dog, which gets on well with children. Its total lack of aggression does not prevent it from being an excellent guard dog. One has to point out that it is not very good at accepting commands. Despite its origin it has adapted to the problems of urban life and living indoors. However as any Spitz, which in addition is a faithful heir of the northern wolf, the Samoyed does not feel happy when it is shut in confined premises.

All year round, it likes playing in water, but is very sensitive to heat.

For thousands of years the Canadian Eskimo Dog was used by Inuits for pulling a sledge in the north of Canada, above the Hudson Bay. It shows a distinctly independent nature which causes

Samoyed, Canadian Eskimo Dog

it to fight with other members of the pack for the position of pack leader. It requires strict training in order to accept a human as pack leader, and even though it tolerates his presence, it is first and foremost a working dog.

The tail of the Canadian Eskimo Dog is thick and curled to the side.

Thanks to the very dense fur between the toes the Samoyed moves very well in snow. During a snow storm it covers its snout with its thick tail.

Due to the upward curve in their lips the Samoyeds look as if they are smiling.

Hunting Dogs

The Basset Hound comes from North America. It has a very old origin, possibly the result of crossing the Basset and Bloodhound, hence its name. In the past it was used as a pack hunting dog, now it is employed more as a *gun-toting* dog.

Presumably people knew and appreciated this breed long ago because it is referred to by Shakespeare, and General La Fayette gave one to Washington! Thanks to its very developed sense of smell, it is an excellent hunter, used in the United States also as a companion dog. However, it is always better if the Basset Hound is provided with a large area, because it is an active animal. It is stubborn and does not always get on well with strangers or befriend them.

Hounds

The Basset Fauve de Bretagne was developed

by crossing the Griffon Fauve de Bretagne and Basset Griffon Vendeen. It is an old breed of pack hound, specializing in chasing fur game. Even though it is used to the life of a hunter, it is a placid and peaceful dog which adapts to confined areas and can be valued also as a companion dog.

The St. Hubert Hound or Bloodhound is of Belgium nationality. It is a very old breed whose origin probably dates back to the 7th century, when it was taken to Arden. Undoubtedly, it is the oldest hound, which was used for coursing by *King Louis*. There are lots of interpretations of the actual word *Bloodhound* and they are quite controversial: "it chases the prey even after death," "pure-blooded dog" or "royal court dog." This breed was given its English name at the key moment of the Norman Conquest under William the Conqueror. A legend from the 18th century is told about this hound that it was named after St. Hubert, the patron of St. Hubert's Abbey and the then Lord of Aquitaine, who received divine inspiration and entered holy orders but did not want to part from his favorite black dogs.

He became Bishop of Liège and kept a pack of his dogs in the monastery. After his death, monks named the dogs after their master.

This hound is an ancestor of a great number of French dogs. For a long time it has been one of the best hounds, with a very acute sense of smell. Thanks to this excellent quality it is an outstanding tracker, capable of following up a scent and that is why it is successfully used as a police dog. It is one of the most efficient hounds, even though it is not very fast. Despite its illustrious noble history, this dog is an obedient and pleasant companion, and very popular in England and the United States.

The Griffon Fauve de Bretagne is not very common outside the territory of France. It has short legs, is of a rustic and not very elegant appearance, with a shaggy and untidy coat as other Griffons. This dog is stubborn, clever and courageous; it was able to bravely stand up to wolves. Today, it is a hound used for hunting small game: rabbits, foxes or wild boar. Moreover, it excels as a brilliant companion, always in a good mood, patient and placid with children, although very independent.

Beagle [1], Basset Fauve de Bretagne [2] and Griffon Fauve de Bretagne [3].

The Briquet Griffon Vendéen is of French nationality. Contrary to many other hounds it has a long shaggy coat and bushy beard. It is fast and tenacious and has all the qualities of a hunting dog. It enjoys solitude as well as the presence of its master, thus making it an ideal companion. This dog is very likeable, has a lively look and its behavior is also very sweet. It is affectionate and docile so it will be an excellent pet and will not be depressed, if it does not run for three hours a day!

The Beagle is of English nationality. It is a very old breed whose origin probably dates back to ancient times. It has a characteristic range of low bark, beautiful color of coat and intelligence, thanks to which it is one of the shrewdest hounds of the group. Moreover, it is the smallest of these dogs which does not prevent it from hunting large and small game. It is bold and relentless. The Beagle is very popular in the United States, where it hunts hares, wild boar, foxes and deer. It also participates in competitions at dog tracks. It behaves as an excellent companion dog; it is playful and attached to its family.

With its balanced body, the Beagle resembles a miniature Foxhound. It is sturdy and muscular, radiating strength and energy.

Although the drooping ears of the Basset Hound get in the way while eating and drinking, they are very useful, when it needs to pick up a scent, mainly on damp mornings.

The Basset Hound is a dog of comical appearance par excellence, three times longer than tall, with a huge head, sadly drooping ears. Something serious and disenchanted in its eyes makes it seem like a sad clown.

285

Do not believe its clumsy appearance and sad eyes: the Basset Hound is the best at hunting, where its tough nature, tenacity and agility perform wonders.

The coat of this dog is short and smooth, covering the loose and extremely folded skin.

The Briquet Griffon Vendéen is a harmonious miniature of the Grand Griffon Vendéen. Its bushy and rough coat can be of a single color – in light shades – white, fawn or sandy – or three colors, where white and fawn are combined with black.

The Basset Fauve de Bretagne is of a strong-willed nature. Its body consists predominantly of bones and muscles; it is of fawn color, preferably of the gold-wheaten or lively red-wheaten shades. The hair is very stiff, rough and quite short.

The hard coat of the Griffon Fauve de Bretagne protects it against thorny plants of the Breton moor land. The color of its coat ranges from the color of ripened corn to red.

This Griffon, which is purely a Breton product, is of strong personality. Its bravery and valor are legendary, as well as its rebellious and independent spirit.

293

The St. Hubert Hound has a huge head: a high and pointed skull, loose skin with deep wrinkles on the cheeks and forehead, very drooping jowls with overdeveloped dewlaps. Thanks to its thoughtful and melancholic appearance it will immediately win your heart.

The shiny black coat
of the Gordon Setter has
lots of admirers.

The English Setter, undoubtedly a British dog, has all the properties of a Setter: it is beautiful, fast, elegant and it is an excellent pointing breed. It specializes in hunting woodcock, probably the most difficult game bird to hunt, owing to its coloring, which completely blends in with the environment. Its task is simplified by its well-developed sense of sight and smell.

The English Setter is first and foremost a hunting dog, which appeared at the point when hunting rifles started being used. Its fame spread worldwide by 1860 and in 1880 it was brought to France. It is the most often used pointing breed. However, it is advisable to train it as a puppy to come when called. If its destiny is to be a companion dog, a task which this breed can perform excellently, it is necessary to respect its needs and its desire for space and movement. By various crossings, two varieties were developed in Great Britain: one larger and more elegant, aimed more at competi-

tions, and the second having a smaller body and being more sporty, suitable for hunting.

The Gordon Setter is of English origin and a Scottish breed, which was developed by Alexander Gordon, Fourth Duke of Richmond at the beginning of the 19th century. Its blood has a bit of Big Spaniel, Black Setter, Collie, Irish Setter and some of the St. Hubert Hound in it. This Setter does not display as much elegance as its relatives, it is more rustic, but yet at the same time it is an excellent long-distance runner as well as a good guard. It is content in various terrains (woods, marshland, plains) and has an excellent sense of smell. When it stops, it will set waiting for the orders of its master. In addition the Gordon Setter excels as a tremendous companion. It is easy to train and is very much appreciated for its coat and good character.

Setters

When born, Setters
(here the English Setter)
usually have a white coat.
Colors appear gradually
and shades intensify
from the 2nd to 3rd month.

The Gordon Setter is of robust constitution and is very agile, resilient to exhaustion and displays great effectiveness in hunting.

The big chest of this dog enables it to make use of a large respiratory capacity.

The coat of the Gordon Setter is medium long, straight without waves and shorter and finer on the head and front parts of legs.

303

The Wiemaraner
is well known for its
strength and agility.

The Wiemaraner is of German nationality. However one must not confuse this dog with the Deutscher Wachtelhund. Its origin is very controversial. It may have a lot or little of the Saint-Louis Hound, St. Hubert Hound or some of the German pointers in it. Without doubt one may say it is a very old dog, which is at the same time elegant, well muscled and imposing.

A small amusing detail: the short-haired variety has a shortened tail, which on the large dog body creates a comical sight. It is most of all a hunting dog with an excellent sense of smell and very good setter's skills. Thanks to its coat – the shade of which changes as the light hits it – its speed and ability to quickly and silently move forward, it has been nicknamed the "Grey Phantom" in the United States, where it is used by some police forces. However this breed needs to be brought up properly to be able to live in human company.

The Deutscher Wachtelhund is extremely popular in its country. Its ancestors definitely included the Spanish Pointer and the Pointer. It is one of the best breeds of this group. It is fast, adapts to various terrains and has a remarkable sense of smell. This dog is beautiful and efficient, so it has all the prerequisites to be liked, and is sought after also for its qualities as an excellent companion for a family and children – under the condition you respect its distinctive liking for long walks in the fresh air. Some of these dogs display shyness, particularly the wire-haired variety.

Pointers

The Hungarian Pointer was developed by crossing the Hungarian Vizsla and Yellow Turkish Hunting Dog of the 18th century. It survived World War II thanks to expatriation of some Hungarians in the 1930s. To begin with, it was a pointing and retrieving dog and today it is a companion dog boasting excellent health.

The German Short-haired Pointer, which is also called Kurzhaar (which means "rough coat" in German) is a favorite among German and British hunters.

The Hungarian Pointer is a hunting dog of medium size with rough, thick and slick hair.

The Wiemaraner was used in Germany by Grand Dukes of Sachsen-Weimar in the 17th century for deer and wild boar hunting.

The Wiemaraner is sensitive to noise. These dogs bark only rarely but with a strong voice.

The Wiemaraner has a rigid, very thick and shiny coat of silvery grey, brownish grey or mouse grey color and all shades in between.

The blue eyes of the Wiemaraner puppies [1, 2, 3 and 4] will change into amber yellow at the age of 3 months. Right from the start, puppies are very active and try to chew anything in reach of their jaws.

The Long-haired Wiemaraner [5, 6], a rarer variety than the short-haired dog, is distinguished with a prominent nape, thanks to which it seems to carry its head in a majestic way.

317

The Brittany is the most French pointing breed. Its distant ancestor is the "Bird Dog," which is referred to even by Gaston Phébus, Count of Foix, in the 14th century. Its French name épagneul is probably derived from the word *s'espanir* or *s'espaignir* (from French or Occitan language), which probably meant "to lie."

The Spaniel was probably a dog that used to lie on the ground covering the game. But that is only one of the hypotheses relating to its name. It has remained a favorite companion of French hunters; it is intelligent, mischievous and affectionate, sensitive, solid and resilient. It prefers hunting woodcocks and pheasants, which it can track thanks to its remarkable sense of smell.

The French Spaniel is probably also the offspring of "Bird Dogs" of Gaston Phébus. Even though it is a typical French breed, it is less so than the Brittany, and its reputation goes beyond European borders. Its temperament is similar to the Setter's. It is an excellent pointing dog, which moves in a zigzag fashion. It tracks all large and small game including birds in any terrain, where it carries out tasks as a pointing and retrieving dog.

The English Springer Spaniel is the most direct offspring of the Spaniels used in the 17th century and was named for its amazing skills in springing after game. One has to point out that for this purpose it has very strong shoulders and quite long legs. This hound excels with a loyal and meek temperament. As all dogs of this category, it wags its tail a lot. The English Springer Spaniel is very sociable and adores children.

Spaniel and Springer Spaniel

The Welsh Springer Spaniel displays great versatility. It is particularly gifted in wild fowl hunting. This dog is especially resilient and can hunt in all types of terrain in any weather conditions. It is also used as a sheepdog. The Welsh Springer Spaniel is an independent and sensitive dog which is easy to train.

The Brittany, which comes from Bretagne [left and following double spread], was crossed with Setters, Pointers and British Springer Spaniels in the 19th century.

The Springer Spaniel is a fast dog full of energy; it needs a large space and a lot of exercise.

The Brittany, rivalled by English
dogs, escaped extinction in
the 19th century thanks to
an abbot who was interested
in hunting and managed to
restore the breed to the
shape it is known as now.

The Welsh Springer Spaniel, which was often confused with the Welsh Cocker Spaniel, was recognized as a breed in 1902.

The Cocker Spaniel,
the star of Spaniels,
is equipped with great
strength in a small
frame.

The Cocker Spaniel is the most popular of English small Spaniels. It is also a dog popular all over the world. Its ancestors, as with all other Spaniels, include Spanish dogs. It is known that this breed was taken to France as early as the 14th century, because it is referred to by Gaston Phébus, Count of Foix in his booklet "Chiens d'Oysel" (Bird Dogs).

Long ears covered with woolly hair, a gentle look and a charming temperament are the reasons why owners, which this dog has wrapped round its little "finger," adore it. Originally, it was a hunting dog with excellent pointing skills and not a companion or three times with its long eye-lashes, having at the same time a gentle and roguish look, all is forgiven.

The Rhodesian Ridgeback comes from South Africa. This tracker of felines is capable of hunting in extreme conditions, whether it concerns climate or terrain. It copes well with lack of water and food.

The Pointer of English nationality is one of the best examples of a pointing breed. Its ancestors proba-

Cocker Spaniel, Rhodesian Ridgeback, Pointer,
Korthals Griffon, Karelian Bear Dog, Norwegian Puffin Dog

breed. Its speciality in France and Great Britain is woodcock hunting. The Cocker Spaniel is valued also as a companion dog, but it needs a lot of exercise and is not very keen on the company of children. This dog is cunning and seductive and when it blinks two bly included the English Pointing Dog, French Pointing Dog and Portuguese Pointing Dog. This very ingenious crossing resulted in a dog combining many excellent qualities: beauty, nobility, intelligence and brilliant hunting skills.

This hound is an aristocrat among the breeds, a pointing and retrieving dog. Moreover, it also boasts remarkable athletic skills; it is placid with children and very courageous. If its master respects its need for exercise and large areas it can be an excellent companion dog.

The Korthals Griffon, which was developed by the Dutch, is an outstanding retrieving dog. This pointing hound is a mixture of the Griffon, Setter, Spaniel, Otterhound and Deutscher Wachtelhund. Since it inherited the qualities of all these dogs, it is a versatile hound, and hunters like using the various abilities of this dog, which remains a champion in hare and quail hunting.

[1 and 2] The Karelian Bear Dog hunts Scandinavian elks, bears and wild boar. Its black and white coat sharply contrasts with most of the Nordic Spitz breeds.

[3, 4 and 5] The Norwegian Puffin Dog once climbed the steep slopes of Norway to chase puffins. Its body is adapted to this task. It has six toes on each paw, wide pads, double dewclaws and very flexible vertebrae.

The Korthals Griffon can look like a grouch, but with its beard, moustache and distinctive eyebrows it seems likeable. Most often it is chestnut brown or steel grey with chestnut markings, but it can also be greyish red.

The Rhodesian Ridgeback,
which was developed by the Boers,
has a unique quality: a strip
of back-combed hair, making
an arrow along the spine,
hence the name *Ridgeback*.

The Pointer puppies display their abilities right from the very beginning. Some at the age of two months are able to point in a remarkable way, which is characteristic for this breed.

The Pointer, which has been gifted with an excellent sense of smell, perfect memory, extraordinary concentration skills and astonishing perseverance, is a real "pure-blooded" dog for open terrain hunting.

The Cocker Spaniel, whose name is derived from the English word woodcock or cock, is a bit larger than its relative, the American Cocker.

The Cocker Spaniel or English Cocker Spaniel, which astonishes with its exuberance and vitality, learns quickly and requires a lot of affection.

This dog is excellent for hunting, but it is also used for detecting narcotics.

The introduction of the Cocker Spaniel in France in the early 19th century was down to the great enthusiasm for English hunting dogs.

Water Dogs

Swimming is a favourite
sport of the Golden
Retriever.

T he Newfoundland practically has a monopoly on rescue work in the sea and fresh water. It is one of the indigenous breeds of the North American continent. We do not know its exact origin, but at the end of the 17th century it appeared on the Island of Newfoundland. Fishermen trained this dog to bring in nets full of fish.

Its robust and resilient physique along with its composure and sense of initiative make it look at home in the water. The Newfoundland is accustomed to rescuing people from water to such a degree that it will not even allow its master to enjoy himself having fun in the water but will jump in to drag him onto the shore. These qualities are inherent in the breed, but to make the Newfoundland even more efficient, it has to undergo basic training and regular practice sessions. Then it is perfectly capable of jumping from a boat, finding a person, who has difficulties in open sea, grasping his arm in its mouth, and pulling him onto shore.

Moreover, it has to learn to carry out these rescue operations as fast as possible and via the shortest route available. This dog, an instinctive rescuer, is also a courageous and loyal friend to man, whether in danger or not.

The Nova Scotia Duck Tolling Retriever or Toller is an intelligent dog and a powerful swimmer. In Europe it is practically unknown, but in its own country, Canada, the breed is very popular. This

Retriever and Newfoundland

clever, tenacious and easy to train dog is considered more and more to be a companion dog. It shows a loyal and obedient nature, likes being pampered and loves swimming. Moreover, it is necessary to take it for long walks or let it run about freely in open space.

The Curly-Coated Retriever is one of the most beautiful English specimens of a retrieving dog. It is an ingenious mixture of the Labrador, Newfoundland and Poodle. This breed boasts a "star like" appearance. This dog is elegant, distinguished, with a curly coat and long legs; it has a strong personality, although hunters prefer the Flat-Coated Retriever. This pointer-retriever feels as much at home in the water as on land. It is an expert in duck hunting. It has to compete against its rivals, namely the Labrador and Golden Retriever, whose sense of smell is better developed.

The Flat-Coated Retriever is of English nationality. The precise origin of this breed is not known, but the certainty is that it is a product of a crossing between the Labrador and Newfoundland, from which it inherited retrieving abilities. It is mainly a British dog, affectionate, patient, simply a good companion dog. It excels in hunting in all terrains, on the land as well as water.

The Golden Retriever probably comes from the old breed of the Caucasian Mountain Dog, which was trained to perform in the circus, from where it was probably bought by an Englishman in order to cross it with the Bloodhound. In this way the Golden Retriever probably acquired British nationality. Today, all over the world this breed enjoys great popularity similar to that of the Labrador, but in France it is not well known. It is a dog specially gifted in fetching small game, mainly aquatic species. The Golden Retriever is also used as a guide dog and is engaged in work for police forces. It is an affectionate and peaceful dog which has immense patience with children.

When the Flat-Coated Retriever appeared for the first time at a dog show in Great Britain in 1859, the color of its coat resembled that of the Labrador. In the course of a few years it finally acquired its characteristic thick and fine texture.

Training of the Golden Retriever
can start at the age of 2 months.
Its excellent memory makes
this dog highly trainable.

The coat of the Golden Retriever is smooth or wavy with beautiful fringes on the chest, legs and tail.

Although the young Golden Retrievers and Labradors are like two peas in a pod, the Golden Retriever's light golden coat turns into the typical thick and silky fur after 4 – 5 months.

The Golden Retriever
is a symmetrical, robust dog
with energetic behavior.

The Nova Scotia Retriever is used for hunting in a peculiar way: the dog jumps on the river bank within visibility of ducks, and the hunter positioned in a hide-out throws it sticks or a ball. The dog training arouses curiosity in the ducks, which then swim in closer, getting in range of the gun. Subsequently, the Retriever's task is to fetch the dead or injured animals.

As with the other dogs in this group, the Curly-Coated Retriever is also equipped with an exceptional sense of smell and a waterproof coat.

The webbed feet, strong legs and waterproof coat of the Newfoundland allow it to swim even in very cold water for hours.

The obedient puppies of the Newfoundland, which resemble little cuddly toys, weigh at birth between 600 and 800 grams (1½-2 pounds). And yet at the age of 2 months they come up to 10 kilograms (25 pounds). From then on the growth continues at a slower pace. It reaches its maturity at the age of 2 years.

The Labrador of English nationality has an unusual history. It was brought to Newfoundland by the English who then trained it in a special way, transforming its excellent water abilities into land skills: namely to bring the prey to the hunter, which in this case was game and not the loosened nets or the fish that had escaped from nets, as it had together with cod fishermen in the 19th century.

This sturdy, though somewhat oafish and clumsy, dog with a swinging gait evokes strength, resistance and pugnacity. The suitable selection and cross breeding resulted in gaining a breed of a bigger size. The Labrador is versatile; it is a waterdog, retriever, drug sniffing dog, guide dog and companion. It is likeable, loyal and attached to members of the household. It needs a lot of exercise.

The Labrador is an acolyte of the Newfoundland. According to legend, the mother of this dog with a fine coat was supposedly an otter. Is this relation the reason for it being such a good swimmer? The

Labrador, which originates from the Canadian Island of Newfoundland, feels comfortable in very cold waters. Its intelligence, diligence and history as a retrieving dog have made it into a valued helper during rescue work at sea. Its skills are enhanced by webbed feet and the so-called "otter's" tail. Thanks to its patience, flexibility and obedience it is a priceless help to physically handicapped people. The Labrador undergoes special

Labrador Retriever

training, where it learns how to pick up a phone, pull a wheelchair, open a door or warn a blind person that a car is approaching at a fast speed. With its well-developed sense of communication it is even capable of passing a shopping list to a local grocer, knowing that its master definitely has not forgotten to put treats on it.

The Labrador's coat, with a waterproof undercoat underneath is completely black, chocolate or a yellow ranging from fox-red to light cream.

The Labrador's physical qualities make it an excellent swimmer: a short and waterproof coat, a tail which, with its round shape resembles that of an otter, round and compact paws.

Solidly built, a little stocky, the Labrador has a wide head and strong legs.

The Labrador has a remarkably balanced temperament and that is the reason why it has become successful internationally.

A Labrador puppy grows
much faster than others
and can be trained
for any task.

From an early age
the Labrador shows great
pleasure in frolicking in water.

Very attached to man,
the Landseer manifests
an excellent aptitude
for rescuing.

The Landseer (the Continental-European type) is considered by Great Britain and Canada to be just a variety of the Newfoundland, while the international cynology organization - Fédération Cynologique Internationale (FCI) recognized it as an individual breed as early as 1960. It originates from Canada and displays the same qualities and skills as the Newfoundland.

It was probably taken to Newfoundland by Basque and Portuguese fishermen, who crossed their mastiffs and water dogs with local breeds. It was named in a quite original way, after the animal painter Sir Edwin Landseer, who made it immortal in a painting in 1837. At the beginning of the 20th century the Landseer evaded extinction thanks to German breeders, who crossed it with mountain dogs. It is a breed specially gifted in fishing, hunting of aquatic game and water activities in general. It is a good companion dog, valued for its intelligence and amicable temperament.

The Irish Water Dog's ancestors include, among others, the Irish Water Spaniels. It was developed by crossing the Poodle with Irish Setters or the Curly-Coated Retrievers in the 19th century. It boasts excellent skills in retrieving water game and is talented mainly in hunting wild ducks in marshland or lakes.

The Frisian Water Dog or in Dutch, **Wetterhoun**, has lived in Holland for three centuries, where it at one time hunted otters. It is sturdy and tough; it retrieves game on land as well as in water.

Landseer and Water Dogs

The Portuguese Water Dog originates from the province of Algarve. It is an old breed that was used by fishermen for a lot of varied tasks during which boatmen could take advantage of its swimming skills: bringing in nets, passing messages from one boat to another or onshore, catching ropes or guarding boats on the shore.

[1 and 4] The Irish
Water Dog, well
accustomed to the
vigorous climate of
the estuaries of its
country, displays
immense stamina.

[5 and 6] The Frisian
Water Dog, which
is very courageous,
can also behave in
an aggressive and
disobedient way.
It needs an uncom-
promising upbringing.

377

The traditional lion cut of the Portuguese Water Dog (trimming from the end of the rib cage) provides it not only with protection against the cold but also enables it to perform better in water.

The Landseer has webbed feet and a coat with long, smooth and soft hair; less dense than is the coat of the Newfoundland.

The Landseer coat color is pure white with discontinuous black markings on the body and hindquarters.

Watchdogs

The Bullmastiff radiates
strength, but this dog is also
well behaved and obedient.

The Doberman of German nationality is the at the apex of guard and protection dogs. It does not have to try to live up to its reputation. It is enough to catch sight of its sharp teeth and immediately you will stop feeling like messing around with it ...

The origin of this fiercest guard dog is attributed to a tax collector, who at the end of the 19th century used it as a deterrent against irate tax payers ... It was developed by crossing various dogs: **Pinscher, Dogue, Rottweiler;** moreover it is known that the coat color was achieved by crossing it with the Manchester Terrier. The Doberman is a mythical prototype for fighting dogs, a model of a bad and vicious dog, longing for fresh meat. The reality is undoubtedly very different, although in the United States it remains the most valued police dog.

the Bulldog, which undoubtedly provided it with the "strength of a bull." It is a good guard, a police as well as companion dog, if its master can train it well, because it is joyful, intelligent and attached to the house and family. But strangers had better beware of crossing reasonable borders; otherwise they will be sorry...

The Sarplaninac or Illyrian Sheepdog originates from Macedonia and Albania. It is also called Sarpla. It could be the most ferocious watchdog –

Doberman, Bullmastiff, Sarplaninac

The Bullmastiff, also referred to as the English Bullmastiff, is an impressive dog with a wide head, dark snout and piercing eyes. This dog is affectionate and soft-hearted, with a lethargic and indolent side. A long time ago it was crossed with

but only at night. During the day it transforms into a kind doggie that nonetheles can jump at the throat of the first wolf trying to approach its flock of sheep. In its own country it is a greatly valued security dog and herd guard.

The Doberman is an excellent athlete, intelligent, courageous and deeply devoted to its master, but from an emotional point of view this dog is very fragile and touchy. It requires persistent, but sensitive training.

The Sarplaninac boasts a long and dense single color mane of any shade from white to dark brown or even black.

This dog, which in 1929 was recognized as different from the Karst Shepherd, lives predominantly in Albania and Macedonia.

389

The Sarplaninac sheepdog, which is extremely courageous and has awesome teeth, makes even wolves scared. Three dogs of this breed would be able to guard a herd of more than 500 animals and drive a pack of wolves.

Although the Bullmastiff requires a certain authority, it can also be very gentle towards children and is sociable with strangers.

The coat of this dog can be any shade of fawn or red, brindle or solid. There is a black mask on the muzzle.

393

The Bullmastiff was very popular in the times of Richard the Lionheart. It was used as a watchdog, a war and fighting dog. It needs strict training, because without it the Bullmastiff can behave towards strangers in a dangerous way.

The Malinois Belgian Shepherd Dog, a great protector, can be a guard or assistance dog.

T he Rottweiler is also called a German Sheepdog or a "Butcher's Dog." It takes after the Mastiff, the Dogue and some old sheepdogs. It apparently originates from the Molosser breed from the era of the Ancient Greek and Roman Empires. Whether it does or not, a long time ago this breed left southern countries and settled in Switzerland and in the south of Württemberg, where it is very common.

From its ancestors, which were the Mastiffs, it kept its huge bulky body. It possesses unquestionable physical qualities which are enhanced by great intelligence, courage and will. It is a good guard of herds, and excels as a watchdog and protection dog. It loves its family and children, whom it will protect with its life.

The Boxer is of German nationality. Its ancient ancestors, which were also of German origin, once hunted wild boars and bears and also guarded herds. Anybody that has experience with the Boxer will know that it is a little "scatterbrained," exuberant, spirited and playful as well as demonstrative, pulling you down on the ground to show you its love ... It is intelligent and very loyal. It can perfectly manage the security of the house and at the same time act in a gentle fashion. Despite its looks it is also a well-balanced dog.

The Malinois is also called the Belgian Shepherd Dog of Mechelen. During World War II this breed was decimated and restored by crossing those Malinois saved with the Groenendaels, which this dog resembles. Due to its not very accommodating and stubborn temperament, this shepherd is not very easy to handle, but on the other hand the Malinois can be an excellent watchdog and companion.

Rottweiler, Boxer, Malinois and Laekenois Belgian Shepherd Dogs

The Laekenois is the rarest of the four varieties of the Belgian Shepherd Dog. It was named after the Chateau of Laeken, the residence of the Belgian Royal Family.

The Malinois Belgian Shepherd Dog instinctively takes on the role of protector.

The Malinois Belgian Shepherd
Dog (similar to the Tervueren)
has a distinct black coat.

The black mask of the
Malinois resembles
the mask of the
German Shepherd.

The Boxer was a product of crossing the Büllenbeisser, a German dog of the Molosser type, and the Bulldog.

The great popularity of the Boxer can be explained by its characteristic expression and its boundless affection.

405

A Rottweiler puppy with its broad skeleton resembles the adult dog in a scaled-down version. It is not advisable to rely on its cuddly look, because its training is not easy.

The Rottweiler has an impressive jaw and temperament. If you do not know it, it is advisable to stay out of its way.

The Akita Inu is obedient
and loyal, but only
towards its master.

The Akita Inu, from 1931 referred to as the national dog of Japan, originates from a hunting dog of the Akita province on the Island of Honshu in south-eastern Japan. It was bred for hunting large game and also used in dog fights against another Japanese fighting dog, the Tosa.

Aiming at strengthening the breed, these dogs were crossed with western Mastiffs resulting in a reduction of the number of authentic Akitas. Thanks to a movement to save this breed, which was established in the early 20th century, it was possible to restore its original qualities.

an exceedingly consistent upbringing. Otherwise beware of its teeth!

The Cane Corso comes from Sicily, where it was used as a butcher's dog and fought in arenas. It is the offspring of the old Italian cattle herding breed, Cane di Macellaio.

The Fila Brasileiro has, as its name suggests, South American roots. It is a product of crossing among the Molossers brought in by conquerors from the New World, Bulldogs and Mastiffs. The conquistadores used the dogs' greatly developed sense of smell to pursue deserters and Indian slaves. It is an excellent sheepdog and a cruel

Akita Inu and American Akita, Neapolitan Mastiff, Cane Corso and Fila Brasileiro

The Neapolitan Mastiff is of Italian nationality. Most definitely it is the offspring of the Persian Mastiffs. Despite its placid expression and its serious tendency to drool, it is a feared watchdog which can act in a very fierce manner. It needs

watchdog. Its fury can be so intensive that some countries banned this breed in their territory. It is undoubtedly a "competition dog," that does not like the urban environment at all. The Fila Brasileiro prefers large spaces and living in the countryside.

Known since the times of ancient empires in all of the Mediterranean countries, the Neapolitan Mastiff "performed" in arenas as early as the era of the Roman Empire.

411

The Cane Corso's front leg muscles are more distinctive than the muscles on the hind legs.

The Akita Inu is independent, proud and sometimes fiery, and has to be trained strictly, but on the basis of trust.

The Akita Inu is impressive and elegant, it has pricked ears, a spiral curled tail and a face resembling the expression of Japanese aristocrats of the classical era.

The Akita Inu does not avoid
the company of strangers,
but only if its master
is present.

The Fila Brasileiro has an impressive look and characteristic gait, which is at the same time supple and elegant.

The coat of this dog is short and soft and can display any color, the most common being light brindle.

The Fila Brasileiro, the national dog of Brazil, is of a sturdy build, with a wide square head and a large fold of skin under its neck.

The American Akita was developed from Akita Inu dogs, which were brought home by American soldiers after World War II.

423

The well balanced
Leonberg barks only
in the case of imminent
danger.

The very popular German Shepherd Dog is a versatile animal par excellence, a herding dog, dispatch bearer, a rescue, police and guide dog because it has all the qualities and intelligence needed for being able to adapt to all kinds of situations.

This breed is extremely adaptable and when trained well it can be a feared attack and protection dog. Nevertheless, it is also capable of behaving very gently and meekly towards children and displays loyalty and obedience. The German Shepherd can be found helping at any disaster struck area, such as an earthquake, gas leak or

The St. Bernard Dog, wearing the sash of the Red Cross, is in itself a symbol of Switzerland. In the 19th century this breed was brought to fame by Barry (its name in German dialect means "bear"), who rescued about forty people. It is extremely intelligent and thanks to its very acute sense of smell and absolutely remarkable resistance to exhaustion and bad weather, it is the "king" of mountain rescue dogs.

The Leonberger is probably the offspring of Tibetan Mastiffs, or is a product of crossing between the

German Shepherd Dog, St. Bernard Dog, Leonberger, Giant Schnauzer

explosion. Like the Boxer, it can find a casualty, warn its master, sniff out a person in a cooled lava mantle or a thick layer of mud, bark to draw attention to a man under rubble, signal for help, and all this even in pitch darkness.

Newfoundland and St. Bernard Dog. This dog was owned by Napoleon III as well as Bismarck. It is exceptionally meek and loving; a born protector of children, whose company this dog especially seeks.

The German Shepherd Dog was originally bred for guarding sheep in the mountainous regions of Germany. It is sometimes referred to as the "wolf dog," thanks to the great resemblance to its wild relatives.

Despite the German Shepherd's exceptional qualities, this dog, with its dominating character, needs strict training and a master who will teach it obedience.

429

The main disadvantage of the German Shepherd Dog is the fact that it is capable of eating up to two pounds of meat a day!

The Leonberger was named after the small town of Leonberg, where famous breeder Heinrich Essig decided to develop a dog with a golden color in honor of the crest of his town.

434

The St. Bernard Dog is able to find a person covered under several feet of snow and find him at a distance of 150 feet.

435

The St. Bernard Dog is heavy and strong (some can weigh up to 250 pounds). It is one of the largest rescue dogs in the world. Thanks to its wide paws with a high instep this dog moves well in snow.

The Intelligent Giant Schnauzer is easy to train and, owing to its greatly developed sense of smell, was used by armies during both World Wars.

438

In order to develop a dog as large as the Giant Schnauzer (2-3 feet), breeders crossed the Standard Schnauzers with Great Danes and Bouviers des Flandres.

This dog is affectionate, devoted, vigilant, vivacious, but not too boisterous.

441

The German Mastiff is more widely known by the name Great Dane. What was the reason that this dog was nicknamed the "Apollo of Dogs?" Was it because the Great Dane was already known to Ancient Greece or was it a tribute to its great beauty? Its origin is disputed; however everybody agrees that it is one of the most magnificent specimens of the canine race.

This dog has long legs; it is slender and well muscled and displays a great temperament. When guarding a house the Great Dane is capable of jumping at a burglar's throat and killing him in cold blood. However, it is necessary to say that this "aggression" is only temporary: under normal circumstances it is an amiable and well balanced dog.

The Tibetan Mastiff is of English nationality. It is the last representative of the original Molossers. If only because of its ancestry, this dog is of a very strong constitution. The original Tibetan Mastiff still lives in the Himalayas and the bonzes use it for protection. This dog was brought to England and various crossings resulted in developing the British version of the "Tibetan Mastiff." It is a massive animal with imposing teeth and a wide arched head. It is accompanied with the reputation of an aggressive dog, at least the Tibetan variety. The western type is more malleable, less aggressive and better suited for police work.

The Dogue de Bordeaux is of much disputed origin. Is it the offspring of the Mastiffs, Spanish Dogs, Molossers or Dogs of Aquitaine. It resembles a huge Boxer. The same sullen, flat and wrinkled muzzle, the same square head, the same strong musculature and the same deceptively ferocious

Molossers

appearance, since this giant can behave toward children exceptionally gently. Its strength is off-putting and its courage makes it a good police assistant.

When born, the Great Dane admittedly looks like a kitten, but it keeps growing at a frightening rate and an adult dog will reach a size matching a calf.

The very rare **Dogo Argentino** was developed in 1910 by crossing the fighting dog of Cordoba with a number of dogs, which the breeders considered to be the right ones to give this animal the sought-after qualities, namely, sense of smell, balance, courage, strength, size and color. From a distance it resembles a white Labrador. The Dogo, as it is called in Argentina, was used to hunt large animals: pumas, jaguars and wild boars. The qualities of a watchdog and a hunting dog do not prevent it from being a good companion to a family and children. However, it needs to undergo strict training, which will curb its very distinctly independent temperament and will.

445

The Tibetan Mastiff does not rely only on its 200 pounds to scare off intruders.

This Mastiff is
a very impressive
and well balanced
dog. Its long coat
creates a mane,
which can be black,
blue, black or
blue with fawn
markings,
or fawn.

447

The coat of the Dogue de Bordeaux is mahogany or fawn, with a distinctive red or black mask. Faint white markings on the chest or legs are allowed.

The tactful and gentle upbringing of the Dogo Argentino must start at an early age.

451

Index

German Shepherd

Shetland Sheepdog

Bichon Havanese

Bull Terrier

Curly-Coated Poodle

Cocker Spaniel

Alaskan Malamute

J

K

Labrador

Lhassa Apso

Saint Bernard

Nova Scotia Duck Tolling Retriever

Curly-Coated Retriever

Giant Schnauzer

Samoyed

W

X

Welsh Springer Spaniel

Y

[1] Gordon Setter, [2] English Setter, [3] Pekinese, [4] Bullmastiff

Acknowledgement

The photographer Yves Lanceau wishes to express his warm thanks to all the professional and amateur breeders who devoted their time to him. Special acknowledgement obviously goes to my assistants and co-workers: Jérôme Bétant, Guillaume Elwart, Anne-Laure Malgonne, Isabelle Masson-Deblaize, Catherine Thoraval. (My memory is unfortunately not entirely reliable so I wish to ask those that I have forgotten for their forgiveness.)

Agoutin Jean-Claude a Mrs André Eliane
Aubaux Roselyne, Claude and Pierre
Auriant Mr and Mrs
Avilez Antoine
Baille C.
Barbau Robert
Berthold Anita
Bertron Jacques
Bourg Jean-Baptiste
Bourgeois Françoise
Bouvret Yvette
Bruguet Odile
Caillard Denys
Carrier Muriel and Gérard
Casteran Martine
Chaplain Mr et Mme
Chevallier Thierry and Christiane
Clipet Gérard and Marie-Line
Closerie Saint-Nicolas
Coët Bruno
Crouillebois Mr and Mrs
Cuny Marie-France
Damman Brigitte
Danjoux Nady
De Bellescize Frédérique
Decaudin Josiane and Stéphanie
Delanou Cyril
Delaunay Liliane
Denon Valérie
Denoues Emmanuelle
Di Matteo Jacky
Dugue B.
Dupond Ludovic
Easley Mme
Fauchet Brigitte
Galicier Christian
Grappin Pascal
Gravelines Jean
Guillet Andrée and Marcel
Hasbrouck Michel
Heck Bruno
Heger Annick
Hinque Pascal and Mrs
Joubier Evelyne
Juttaud Jeannine
Kluber Gérard
Lambert Alain
Laurent Annick and Michel
Lecacheux Chantal
Le Corre VivianeLeguluche Mrs and Stéphanie
Leith Ross Felicity
Lhuillery Chantal
Lladeres Françoise
Le Paih Thire
Le Pape C.
Moço Florence
Natthorst Martine
O'Connor Ruth and Miss
Payancé Patrick
Pellieux Patrick
Penvern Jean-Yves
Pichon Christophe
Poirier Émilie
Pontiès Anne
Ragonnet Jacques
Ramacciotti Catherine
Rey Rose
Rialland Michel
Ribault William and Simone
Rives Viviane
Rodet Magali
Rouquette
Schevbez Michel
Schloupt Monique and Dominique
Specty Michel
Sydney Guy
Tachon Dominique
Thomas Françoise
Tordu Géraldine
Tribu Mme and Miss
Valérie Marie-Jeanne
Wallois Olivier, Mathilde and Lucas
Zivot Mlle

All photographs
by Yves Lanceau.

[1001 photographs]